D1606825

Ants

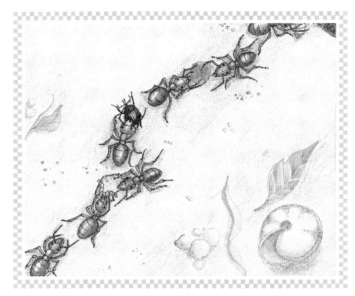

Written by Christine Young
Illustrated by Andrea Jaretzki

RESOURCE ROOM
.... SCHOOL

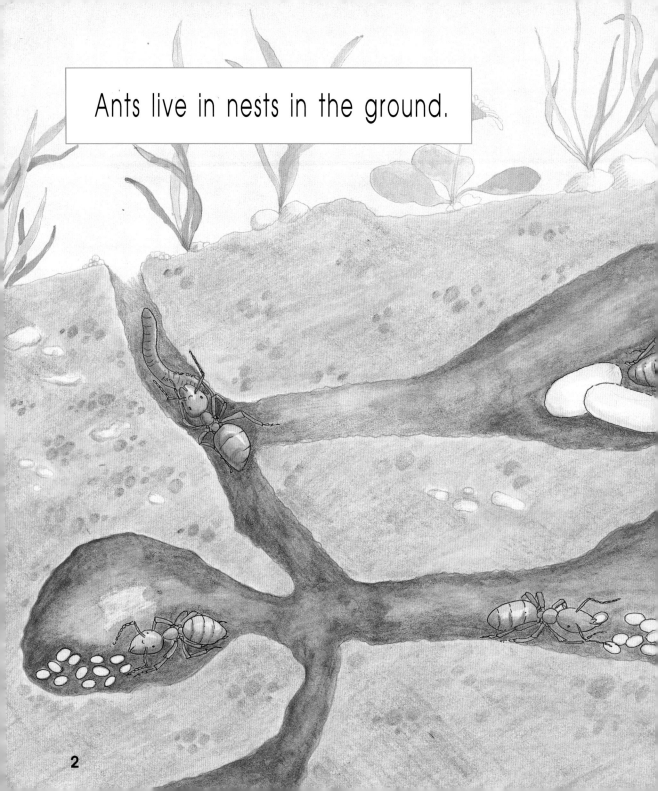

Ants live in nests in the ground.

They make tunnels and rooms. In the rooms, they store food and lay eggs.

3

A queen ant lays the eggs.

4

Soldier ants guard the nests.

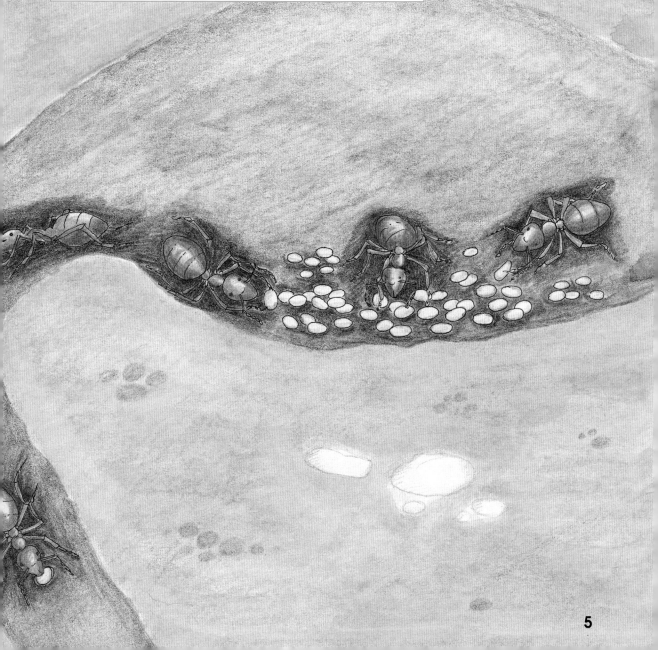

Worker ants gather food,
build the nest,
and look after the baby ants.

Ants march in lines to look for food. They like to eat grubs and beetles. Ants are so strong they can carry other insects back to the nest.

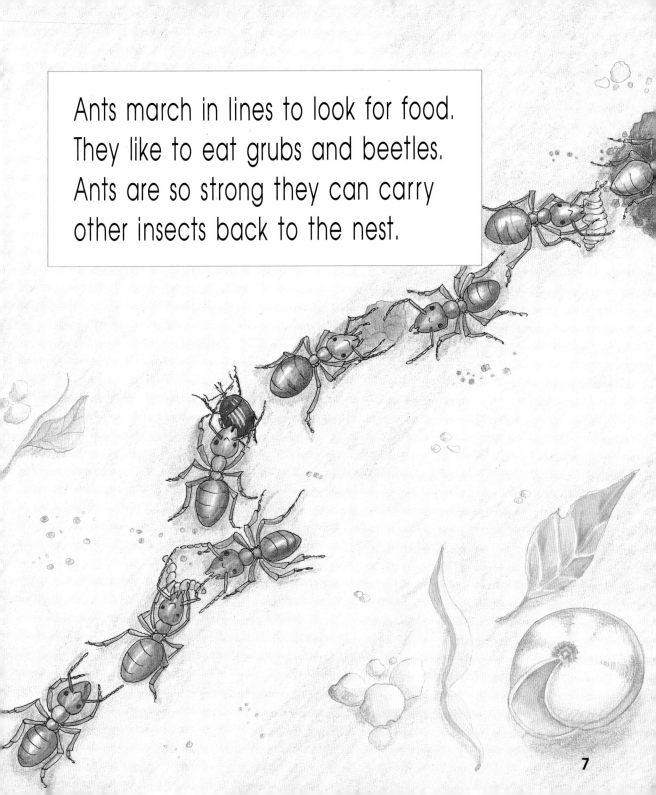

Sometimes, ants don't eat grubs and beetles.
In long lines, they march inside
to eat honey and jam.

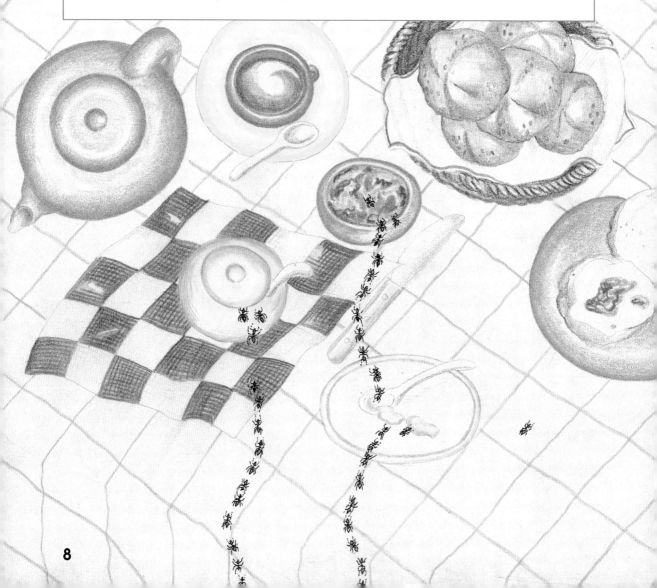